THE

PREMIER LEAGUE ERA:

A QUIZ BOOK FOR

TRUE FOOTBALL FANS

Mark Hope

ISBN: 9798343895483

Contents

Category 1:

The 1990s – The Early Days of the Premier League

1. Which club won the inaugural Premier League season in 1992-1993?

2. Who was the top scorer in the first Premier League season?

3. Which team finished second in the Premier League in 1995-96?

4. Which manager led Blackburn Rovers to the Premier League title in 1994-95?

5. Alan Shearer joined Newcastle United from which club in 1996 for a then-record transfer fee?

6. In what year did Arsène Wenger join Arsenal as manager?

7. Which team was famously relegated on the final day of the 1992-93 season despite

having England international Chris Waddle in their ranks?

8. Who was the first non-British player to score a hat-trick in the Premier League?

9. In what year did Chelsea win their first Premier League title?

10. Who was the first player to score 100 Premier League goals?

11. Which team did Manchester United defeat to secure their famous treble in 1999?

12. Who scored the first-ever Premier League goal?

13. Which player won the PFA Players' Player of the Year award in 1995-96?

14. Who was the only team to beat Manchester United in the 1998-99 Premier League season at Old Trafford?

15. Who was the first non-English manager to win the Premier League?

16. Which striker famously moved from Southampton to Blackburn Rovers for £3.6 million in 1992, making him the most expensive British player at the time?

17. Who scored a hat-trick on his Premier League debut for Leeds United in 1996?

18. Which club was relegated from the Premier League despite finishing with 42 points in 1996-97?

19. Who was the Premier League's leading goal scorer for the 1994-95 season?

20. Which manager famously led Leeds United to the First Division title in 1991-92, the year before the Premier League began?

21. Who was the top scorer in the 1993-94 Premier League season?

22. Which club was the first to be relegated from the Premier League?

23. Who won the Premier League Golden Boot in the 1998-99 season?

24. Which team did Newcastle United beat
5-0 in 1996, with Philippe Albert famously
scoring the fifth goal?

25. In what year did Ruud Gullit become the
first non-British manager to win a major
English trophy, with Chelsea?

26. Who was the last team to win the old
First Division before the creation of the
Premier League?

27. Which future Premier League manager
won the Premier League as a player with
Blackburn Rovers in 1994-95?

28. Who was the Premier League's first
Player of the Month in August 1994?

29. Who was the manager of Arsenal before
Arsène Wenger?

30. Who was the first goalkeeper to save a
penalty in a Premier League match?

Category 2:

The 2000s – Rise of the Giants

1. Who was Arsenal's captain during their unbeaten 'Invincibles' season in 2003-04?

2. Which goalkeeper famously scored a goal in the Premier League for Tottenham Hotspur in 2007?

3. Who became the Premier League's all-time top scorer during the 2000s, a record he still holds?

4. Which club did Roman Abramovich purchase in 2003, changing the dynamics of the Premier League?

5. Cristiano Ronaldo joined Manchester United from which club in 2003?

6. Which club did Arsène Wenger's Arsenal defeat in the 2004-05 FA Cup final, marking Wenger's fourth FA Cup triumph?

7. Who was the top scorer in the Premier League in the 2001-02 season?

8. In 2008, which player won the PFA Players' Player of the Year award while playing for Manchester United?

9. Chelsea won their first Premier League title in the 2004-05 season under which manager?

10. In what year did Manchester City break into the Premier League top four, signalling the start of a new era for the club?

11. Which goalkeeper was famously sent off for handling the ball outside the box in a match between Chelsea and Barcelona in 2000?

12. Who was the first player to score 30 goals in a Premier League season since the league was reduced to 20 teams in 1995?

13. Which Premier League manager famously made the "Special One" comment in 2004?

14. In 2008, who became the first team to go unbeaten at home throughout the entire Premier League season since Arsenal's Invincibles?

15. Which Liverpool player scored 30 goals in the 2007-08 Premier League season, finishing as top scorer?

16. Who was Manchester United's record signing in the summer of 2008, arriving from Tottenham Hotspur?

17. Who scored the winning penalty in the 2005 Champions League final for Liverpool?

18. Which two teams contested the first-ever all-English Champions League final in 2008?

19. Who was Arsenal's leading goal scorer during their 2003-04 Invincibles season?

20. Which manager led Tottenham Hotspur to their first top four finish in the Premier League era in 2009-10?

Category 3:

The 2010s – Dominance of the Top Six

1. Who scored the famous stoppage-time goal that won Manchester City the 2011-12 Premier League title?

2. Which club famously won the Premier League in 2015-16, defying 5000-1 odds?

3. Who was the top scorer in the 2013-14 Premier League season, despite not winning the title?

4. What year did Sir Alex Ferguson retire as manager of Manchester United?

5. Which goalkeeper won the Premier League Golden Glove award in the 2017-18 season?

6. Which club did Liverpool defeat to win the 2019 Champions League final, after losing the Premier League title by a single point?

7. What was Manchester City's points tally when they set a Premier League record by winning the 2017-18 title?

8. Who scored the first-ever goal at Tottenham Hotspur's new stadium in 2019?

9. Which manager led Chelsea to Premier League titles in 2014-15 and 2016-17?

10. Who won the Premier League Golden Boot in both the 2018-19 and 2019-20 seasons?

11. Which manager led Leicester City to their famous Premier League title in the 2015-16 season?

12. Who won the Premier League Golden Boot in 2015-16, scoring 25 goals?

13. In 2013, who was the last player to win the Ballon d'Or while playing in the Premier League?

14. Which club set the record for the most goals scored in a Premier League season in 2017-18?

15. Who won the Premier League Player of the Year award in the 2016-17 season?

16. What was the final score in the 2019 UEFA Champions League final between Liverpool and Tottenham?

17. Which player scored Manchester City's 100th goal of the 2017-18 Premier League season?

18. Who won the Premier League Player of the Month award in December 2018?

19. In 2011, which striker moved from Newcastle United to Liverpool for £35 million, then a British transfer record?

20. Who won the PFA Players' Player of the Year award for the 2018-19 season?

21. Which player won the PFA Young Player of the Year award in both 2016 and 2017?

22. Who scored the first goal of the 2017-18 Premier League season?

23. Which club was promoted to the Premier League for the first time in their history in 2018?

24. Who was the top scorer in the 2011-12 Premier League season?

25. Which team did Manchester City defeat 6-1 on the final day of the 2017-18 season to reach 100 points?

26. Who won the Premier League Golden Boot in the 2015-16 season?

27. Which team did Arsenal beat 5-2 in back-to-back seasons in 2011-12 and 2012-13?

28. Who was the Premier League's top assist provider in the 2019-20 season?

29. Which Premier League club reached the Europa League final in 2017, only to lose to Manchester United?

Category 4:

The 2020s – Modern Era

1. Who won the Premier League title in the 2020-21 season?

2. Which club was relegated from the Premier League in 2021 after spending 16 seasons in the top division?

3. Which player broke the Premier League record for most assists in a single season, with 20, in 2020?

4. Who won the Premier League Golden Boot in the 2021-22 season?

5. Who scored the winning goal in the 2022 FA Cup final?

6. Who was the manager of Aston Villa during their Premier League survival on the final day of the 2019-20 season?

7. Who became Manchester United's all-time top scorer in the Premier League during the 2020-21 season?

8. Who was awarded the Premier League Manager of the Month award for September 2021?

9. Who scored a hat-trick for Manchester United against Leeds United on the opening day of the 2021-22 season?

10. Which Premier League club secured European football for the first time in their history in the 2020-21 season?

11. Which player won the Premier League Player of the Season award for the 2021-22 season?

12. Who scored Manchester City's third goal in their 4-1 win over Brighton in May 2022, which secured their 2021-22 Premier League title?

13. Who became the first player to score 100 Premier League goals for Liverpool?

14. Which team finished fourth in the 2021-22 Premier League season, securing Champions League football?

15. Which team was promoted to the Premier League in the 2022-23 season after a 23-year absence?

16. Who won the Premier League Golden Glove in the 2020-21 season?

17. Which manager guided Leeds United to Premier League promotion in 2020?

18. Who scored the winning goal in the 2021 FA Cup final between Chelsea and Leicester City?

19. Who scored the first goal in Brentford's 2-0 win over Arsenal on the opening day of the 2021-22 Premier League season?

20. Who was the top scorer in the 2022-23 Premier League season?

21. Which club finished 4th in the 2022-2023 Premier League season, qualifying for the Champions League?

22. Who was named Premier League Player of the Season for 2022-2023?

23. Which team won the Premier League Golden Glove award for the cleanest sheets in the 2020-2021 season?

24. Which manager replaced Graham Potter at Chelsea during the 2022-2023 Premier League season?

25. Who scored a record-breaking 36 goals in the 2022-2023 Premier League season?

26. Which Premier League club was promoted in the 2022-2023 season and achieved a top-half finish in their first season back?

27. Who was the youngest player to score a Premier League hat-trick in the 2020s?

28. Who was the Premier League Manager of the Season for 2022-2023?

Category 5:

Iconic Players and Managers

1. Which manager has won the most Premier League titles?

2. Who was the first player to score 30 goals in a Premier League season?

3. Which player holds the record for the fastest Premier League hat-trick, scored in 2 minutes and 56 seconds?

4. Which manager guided Arsenal to a record 49-game unbeaten run in the Premier League?

5. Who was Chelsea's captain during their back-to-back Premier League title wins in 2004-05 and 2005-06?

6. Which midfielder holds the record for the most Premier League assists in a single season?

7. Who is the highest-scoring non-European player in Premier League history?

8. Which player has made the most appearances in Premier League history?

9. Which player has scored the most goals in Premier League London derbies?

10. Which player was named Premier League Player of the Season in both 2017 and 2018?

11. Which manager won back-to-back Premier League titles with Manchester City in 2018 and 2019?

12. Which goalkeeper has saved the most penalties in Premier League history?

13. Which player holds the record for the most Premier League appearances as captain?

14. Who was the first player to score 50 Premier League goals for two different clubs?

15. Who was the first manager to win the Premier League four times in a row?

16. Which player has won the most Premier League titles?

17. Who was the first goalkeeper to keep 100 clean sheets in the Premier League?

18. Who holds the record for the most consecutive wins as a Premier League manager?

Category 6:

Records and Statistics

1.Which team holds the record for the most consecutive Premier League wins in a single season?

2.Who was the youngest player to score a Premier League goal?

3.Which player has received the most red cards in Premier League history?

4.Who holds the record for the fastest goal in Premier League history?

5.Who holds the record for the most assists in a single Premier League season?

6.Which team has recorded the longest unbeaten run in Premier League history?

7.Who is the oldest player to have played in the Premier League?

8.Who holds the record for the most appearances as a substitute in the Premier League?

9. Who was the first player to score a perfect hat-trick (left foot, right foot, and header) in the Premier League?

10. Which player has scored the most headed goals in Premier League history?

11. Who was the youngest player to captain a Premier League team?

Category 7:

Memorable Matches

1. What was the score in the famous "Aguerooooo" match between Manchester City and QPR in 2012?

2. What was the scoreline in Manchester United's record 9-0 win over Ipswich Town in 1995?

3. Which team came back from 4-0 down to draw 4-4 with Arsenal in 2011?

4. What was the final score in the famous Manchester derby in October 2011, when Manchester City defeated Manchester United at Old Trafford?

5. Who scored the winning goal in Chelsea's 4-3 victory over Liverpool in the 2008 Champions League semi-final?

6. Which team beat Manchester City 3-2 on the final day of the 2012-13 season to ensure they stayed in the Premier League?

7. In which year did Arsenal come from 2-0 down to beat Tottenham 5-2 at the Emirates Stadium?

8. Which Premier League team recorded the largest away win in Premier League history?

9. Who scored the equalizing goal for Crystal Palace in their 3-3 draw with Liverpool in 2014, which effectively ended their title challenge?

10. Who scored all four goals for Liverpool in their 4-3 victory over Leeds United in the opening match of the 2020-21 season?

11. Which player scored the decisive goal in Tottenham's 3-2 win over Ajax in the 2019 Champions League semi-final?

12. Which player scored the opening goal in Manchester City's 6-0 victory over Watford in the 2019 FA Cup final?

Category 8:

Transfers and Signings

1. Which Premier League club broke the British transfer record in 2021, signing Jack Grealish for £100 million?

2. Who was the most expensive defender in Premier League history after his 2019 transfer to Manchester United?

3. Who became the Premier League's most expensive signing in 2016 when Manchester United signed him for £89 million?

4. Which player did Arsenal sign for a club-record £72 million in 2019?

5. Which club signed Fernando Torres from Liverpool for a then British record transfer fee of £50 million in 2011?

6. Who was Manchester City's first £50 million signing in 2015?

7. Which player did Manchester United sign for £75 million from Everton in 2017?

8. Which Premier League club signed Bruno Fernandes in January 2020?

9. Which French midfielder returned to Chelsea from AS Monaco in 2017 for a reported fee of £40 million?

10. Who was Liverpool's record signing in January 2018, joining from Southampton for £75 million?

11. Which striker did Tottenham Hotspur sign for £14 million from Bayer Leverkusen in 2015?

Category 9:

International Influence

1. Which African player won the Premier League with Chelsea in 2004-05 and 2005-06?

2. Which South Korean player was the first to score 50 Premier League goals?

3. Who was the first African player to win the Premier League Player of the Month award?

4. Who was the first African player to captain a Premier League side?

5. Which player scored a hat-trick in Chelsea's 4-2 victory over Tottenham in the 2012 FA Cup semi-final?

6. Who scored the decisive goal for Arsenal in their 5-4 victory over Tottenham Hotspur in the 2004-05 North London Derby?

7. In what year did the Manchester Derby result in a 6-1 victory for Manchester City at Old Trafford?

8. Who scored the only goal in the 2017 Merseyside Derby at Anfield?

9. Which Premier League player scored a hat-trick in the 2020 London Derby between West Ham United and Tottenham Hotspur?

Category 10:

Premier League Goalkeepers

1. Which goalkeeper holds the Premier League record for the cleanest sheets?

2. Who was the first goalkeeper to score a Premier League goal?

3. Which goalkeeper made the most saves in a single Premier League season (2013-14)?

4. Who was Manchester United's goalkeeper during their 2008 Premier League and Champions League double-winning season?

5. Who won the Premier League Golden Glove in the 2019-20 season?

6. Which Premier League goalkeeper saved a record five penalties in a single season in 2019-20?

7. Which goalkeeper was the first to captain a Premier League team in an FA Cup final?

8. Who was Arsenal's first-choice goalkeeper during their 'Invincibles' season in 2003-04?

9. Who kept a clean sheet for Leicester City in their title-clinching game against Everton in 2016?

10. Which goalkeeper won the Premier League Golden Glove for four consecutive seasons (2004-2008)?

11. Who was Tottenham Hotspur's first-choice goalkeeper during their 2018-19 Champions League campaign?

12. Who was the first goalkeeper to reach 150 clean sheets in the Premier League?

13. Which goalkeeper was famously chipped by David Beckham from the halfway line in 1996?

14. Which goalkeeper has the most Premier League saves in a single match (14)?

15. Who was Manchester City's goalkeeper when they won their first Premier League title in 2012?

16. Who was the first goalkeeper to score a Premier League goal with a header?

17. Which Premier League goalkeeper won the Golden Glove award three seasons in a row from 2008 to 2010?

18. Who was Chelsea's starting goalkeeper during their 2004-05 Premier League title-winning season?

19. Which goalkeeper made his Premier League debut for Liverpool in 2018, helping them reach the Champions League final that year?

20. Who was Arsenal's starting goalkeeper during their 1997-98 Premier League title-winning season?

Category 11:

Premier League Captains

1. Who captained Chelsea to their first Premier League title in 2005?

2. Which player captained Manchester City to their 2011-12 Premier League title?

3. Who was Arsenal's captain during their 'Invincibles' season in 2003-04?

4. Who was the youngest captain in Premier League history, captaining West Ham United at just 20 years old?

5. Who was Liverpool's captain during their 2019-20 Premier League title-winning season?

6. Which player captained Leicester City to their incredible Premier League title in 2015-16?

7. Who was the captain of Tottenham Hotspur when they reached the 2019 Champions League final?

8. Who was the first non-British player to captain a Premier League-winning team?

9. Who was Aston Villa's captain during their promotion back to the Premier League in 2019?

10. Who was the captain of Blackburn Rovers during their 1994-95 Premier League title-winning season?

11. Which player captained Chelsea to their 2012 Champions League victory?

12. Who was captain of Leicester City when they won the Premier League in 2015-16?

13. Who was the first non-British captain to lift the Premier League trophy?

14. Who was the captain of Liverpool when they won the Premier League in 2020?

15. Which player was captain of Arsenal during their 2005 FA Cup final win over Manchester United?

16. Who was Everton's captain during the 2019-20 Premier League season?

17. Who captained Manchester United in their famous 1999 Champions League final victory over Bayern Munich?

18. Who captained Wolverhampton Wanderers during their 2019-2020 UEFA Europa League campaign?

Category 12:

Premier League Promotions and Relegations

1. Which club holds the record for the most Premier League promotions?

2. Who was the first team to be relegated from the Premier League in 1993?

3. Which manager guided Wolverhampton Wanderers to promotion to the Premier League in 2018?

4. Which club set the record for the most points in a Championship season when they were promoted to the Premier League in 2006?

5. Which team was promoted to the Premier League in 2021 for the first time in their history?

6. Which club has suffered the most relegations from the Premier League?

7. Which team survived relegation on the final day of the 2019-20 season?

8. Who was the first club to be promoted to the Premier League after winning the Championship play-off final?

9. Which manager famously kept Leicester City in the Premier League in 2014-15, setting the stage for their title win the following year?

10. Which team was relegated in 2022 after spending 16 consecutive seasons in the Premier League?

11. Which club was relegated from the Premier League in the 2019-20 season after just one season in the top flight?

12. Which manager guided Leeds United to promotion to the Premier League in 2020?

13. Who was the first player to score a Premier League goal for Brentford in their debut season in 2021-22?

14. Which Premier League club was relegated in 2016 after spending more than 40 years in the top division?

15. Which team was promoted to the Premier League in 2017 after winning the Championship play-off final?

16. Which club secured Premier League promotion in 2019 after finishing second in the Championship?

17. Which team was promoted to the Premier League in 2021 after winning the Championship title?

18. Who was the first club to win the Premier League after being promoted from the Championship the previous season?

19. Which team was relegated from the Premier League in the 2017-18 season, marking their second relegation in a decade?

Category 13:

Premier League Stadiums and Crowds

1. Which Premier League stadium has the largest capacity?

2. What is the name of Leicester City's stadium?

3. Which Premier League team plays its home games at the Amex Stadium?

4. Who plays their home games at the Etihad Stadium?

5. What was the first Premier League match played at Tottenham Hotspur's new stadium in 2019?

6. What is the name of Aston Villa's home stadium?

7. Which club's fans are famously known as the "Toon Army"?

8. Which Premier League stadium is located closest to the River Thames?

9. Which Premier League club plays their home games at the London Stadium?

10. Which Premier League club's fans are known as the "Toffees"?

11. Which Premier League stadium is nicknamed "The Theatre of Dreams"?

12. What was the name of Arsenal's previous home stadium before they moved to the Emirates Stadium?

13. Which Premier League stadium is located on the banks of the River Mersey?

14. Which Premier League club plays its home matches at St. Mary's Stadium?

15. Who plays their home games at Selhurst Park?

16. Which club plays its home games at Goodison Park?

17. What is the name of Arsenal's home stadium since 2006?

18. Which club plays their home games at the Brentford Community Stadium?

Category 14:

Premier League Derby Matches

1. What is the name of the derby match between Everton and Liverpool?

2. Who scored the winning goal in the 2018 North London Derby, where Arsenal defeated Tottenham 4-2?

3. What was the score in the infamous "Battle of the Bridge" derby between Chelsea and Tottenham in 2016?

4. Who was the only player sent off in the Manchester Derby in 2001, where Manchester United won 3-1?

5. What was the final score in the 2020 Tyne-Wear Derby between Newcastle and Sunderland?

6. Who scored a hat-trick for Tottenham in their 4-1 win over West Ham in the London Derby in 2017?

7. Which club won the 2020 Merseyside Derby at Goodison Park with a score of 2-0?

8. What was the score in the first-ever Premier League meeting between Manchester City and Manchester United in 1992?

9. Who scored the winning goal in the 2016 Manchester Derby that ended 2-1 in favour of Manchester United?

10. What was the score in the 2017 Merseyside Derby at Anfield, where Liverpool defeated Everton?

11. Who was the only player sent off in the 2011 Manchester Derby where Manchester City defeated Manchester United 6-1?

12. What was the final score in the 2014 North London Derby, where Arsenal beat Tottenham at White Hart Lane?

13. What was the score in the 2018 Tyne-Wear Derby, where Sunderland beat Newcastle United?

14. What was the score in the 2018 Merseyside Derby, where Liverpool defeated Everton with a last-minute winner?

15. Who scored the winning goal for Arsenal in the 2020 FA Cup final against Chelsea?

Category 15:

Premier League Penalties

1.Who holds the record for the most penalties scored in Premier League history?

2.Which goalkeeper has saved the most penalties in Premier League history?

3.Who was the first player to miss a penalty in the Premier League?

4.Which player holds the record for the most penalties taken in a single Premier League season?

5.Who was the first player to score a penalty in the Premier League?

6.Which team holds the record for the most penalties awarded in a single Premier League season?

7.Which player holds the record for the most consecutive penalties scored in the Premier League?

8.Who was the first goalkeeper to save two penalties in a single Premier League match?

9.Which player holds the record for the most penalties scored in a single Premier League season?

10.Who was the youngest player to score a penalty in the Premier League?

11.Which Premier League goalkeeper saved three penalties in a single match in 2019?

12.Which Premier League team holds the record for the most penalties missed in a single season?

13.Which goalkeeper saved a crucial penalty from Jamie Vardy to help Manchester City secure the 2021-22 Premier League title?

14.Who scored the winning penalty in the 2022 FA Cup final for Leicester City?

15.Which Premier League manager holds the record for the most penalty shootout wins in domestic cup competitions?

16.Who was the first player to miss a penalty in a Premier League match in the 2021-22 season?

Category 16:

Premier League Penalty Saves

1. Which goalkeeper holds the record for the most penalty saves in Premier League history?

2. Who was the first goalkeeper to save a penalty in the Premier League?

3. Which Premier League goalkeeper saved two penalties in the same match in 2016?

4. Which goalkeeper saved a penalty from Lionel Messi in the 2012 Champions League but went on to become known for his penalty saves in the Premier League?

5. Who saved a penalty from Pierre-Emerick Aubameyang in the North London Derby in 2019?

6. Which Premier League goalkeeper saved a penalty in a 2020 match between Leicester

City and Manchester United to help his team secure a top-four finish?

7. Who saved a penalty from Steven Gerrard in his final Merseyside Derby appearance?

8. Which goalkeeper saved two penalties from Manchester United in a single Premier League match in 2014?

9. Who was the first goalkeeper to save a penalty in a Premier League match for Manchester City in the 2020-21 season?

10. Which goalkeeper saved a penalty in the final game of the 2021-22 season to help Leeds United avoid relegation?

11. Which goalkeeper saved Harry Kane's penalty in a 2022 Premier League match between Tottenham Hotspur and Wolves?

12. Who was the first goalkeeper to save a penalty in the Premier League 2022-23 season?

13. Which goalkeeper saved a penalty from Kevin De Bruyne during Manchester City's title-winning 2021-22 season?

14. Which goalkeeper saved a penalty from Sergio Agüero in his final season at Manchester City?

Category 17:

Premier League Goal scorers

1. Who is the all-time top goal scorer in Premier League history?

2. Which player holds the record for most goals in a single Premier League season?

3. Who was the first player to score five goals in a single Premier League match?

4. Which player holds the record for the most Premier League goals scored for one club?

5. Who was the youngest player to reach 100 Premier League goals?

6. Which player scored the first ever Premier League hat-trick?

7. Who holds the record for the fastest goal in Premier League history?

8. Which player scored the fastest hat-trick in Premier League history?

9. Who holds the record for the most goals scored by a substitute in a single Premier League match?

10. Who was the first player to score 50 goals for two different Premier League clubs?

11. Which player has scored the most goals in London derbies in Premier League history?

12. Who is the highest-scoring midfielder in Premier League history?

13. Who is the top-scoring African player in Premier League history?

14. Which player holds the record for the most goals scored in Manchester derbies?

15. Who was the first player to score four goals in a Premier League match?

16. Which player has scored the most left-footed goals in Premier League history?

17. Who was the first player to score 20 or more goals in five consecutive Premier League seasons?

18. Which player scored the most goals in the 2020-21 Premier League season?

19. Who was the first non-European player to score 100 Premier League goals?

20. Which player has scored the most goals from outside the box in Premier League history?

Category 18:

Premier League Appearances

1. Who holds the record for the most Premier League appearances?

2. Which goalkeeper has made the most Premier League appearances?

3. Who was the youngest player to make a Premier League appearance?

4. Which player holds the record for the most consecutive Premier League appearances?

5. Who was the youngest player to make 100 Premier League appearances?

6. Who was the oldest outfield player to make a Premier League appearance?

7. Which player has made the most Premier League appearances as a substitute?

8. Who was the first player to make 600 Premier League appearances?

9. Which defender holds the record for the most Premier League appearances?

10. Who was the first goalkeeper to make 300 Premier League appearances?

11. Which player has made the most Premier League appearances for Manchester United?

12. Who was the first outfield player to reach 500 Premier League appearances?

13. Who holds the record for the most Premier League appearances as captain?

14. Which non-British player has made the most Premier League appearances?

15. Who was the first player to make 100 appearances for three different Premier League clubs?

16. Which player has made the most
Premier League appearances without ever
winning the title?

17. Which player has made the most
appearances for a single Premier League
club?

Category 19:

Premier League Players' Age

1. Who was the youngest player to score a goal in the Premier League?

2. Who was the oldest player to score a goal in the Premier League?

3. Who was the youngest player to make a Premier League debut?

4. Who was the youngest player to score a hat-trick in the Premier League?

5. Who was the oldest outfield player to play in the Premier League?

6. Who was the youngest player to reach 100 Premier League appearances?

7. Who was the oldest player to win the Premier League?

8. Who was the youngest player to win the Premier League?

9. Who was the youngest player to provide a Premier League assist?

10. Who was the youngest player to score 20 Premier League goals in a season?

11. Who was the youngest player to score in a Manchester derby?

12. Who was the oldest player to captain a Premier League team?

13. Who was the youngest player to score on their Premier League debut?

14. Who was the youngest player to reach 50 Premier League goals?

15. Who was the youngest player to play in the Premier League for Manchester United?

16. Who was the youngest player to score a Premier League penalty?

17. Who was the youngest goalkeeper to keep a clean sheet in the Premier League?

18. Who was the oldest goalkeeper to keep a clean sheet in the Premier League?

Category 20:

Premier League Players' International Caps

1. Who is the most capped African player in Premier League history?

2. Which Premier League player earned the most caps for Brazil while playing in the league?

3. Who is the most capped non-European player in Premier League history?

4. Which Premier League player earned the most caps for Spain while playing in the league?

5. Who is the most capped English player while playing for Manchester United?

6. Which Premier League player earned the most international caps for Portugal?

7. Who is the most capped South American player in Premier League history?

8. Who is the most capped goalkeeper in Premier League history?

9. Which Premier League player earned the most caps for Germany?

10. Who was the first Premier League player to reach 100 international caps?

11. Which Premier League player earned the most caps for Belgium while playing in the Premier League?

12. Who is the most capped Premier League player for Ireland?

13. Which Premier League player earned the most caps for the Netherlands?

14. Who is the most capped Scottish player in Premier League history?

15. Which Premier League player earned the most international caps for France while playing in the league?

16. Who was the first player to earn 50 international caps while playing in the Premier League?

17. Which Premier League player earned the most caps for Argentina?

18. Who is the most capped African goalkeeper in Premier League history?

19. Which Premier League player earned the most international caps for Italy?

Category 21:

Premier League Attendances

1. Which Premier League stadium has the highest capacity?

2. What is the record for the highest attendance in a Premier League match?

3. Which Premier League club holds the record for the highest average attendance in a single season?

4. What is the record for the lowest attendance in Premier League history?

5. Which club set a Premier League attendance record after moving into a new stadium in 2019?

6. Which stadium hosted the highest-ever attendance for a London derby in the Premier League?

7. What is the highest attendance recorded at the Emirates Stadium (Arsenal's home ground) for a Premier League match?

8. Which Premier League club has recorded the highest average attendance in the 2022-23 season?

9. Which stadium saw the highest attendance for a Merseyside Derby in the Premier League?

10. Which Premier League stadium had the highest attendance for a Manchester derby?

11. What is the record attendance at Stamford Bridge for a Premier League match?

12. Which Premier League club recorded the highest attendance at their home stadium in the 2020-21 season?

13. What is the record attendance at the Etihad Stadium for a Premier League match?

14. Which Premier League stadium has the highest average attendance in London?

15. Which Premier League club had the lowest average attendance in the 2021-22 season?

16. What is the record attendance at Villa Park for a Premier League match?

17. Which Premier League stadium recorded the highest attendance for a London derby in 2022?

18. Which club has the highest-ever attendance for a relegation-decider match in Premier League history?

Category 22:

Most Successful Premier League Managers

1. Which manager has won the most Premier League titles?

2. Who is the most successful foreign manager in Premier League history in terms of titles?

3. Which manager led Chelsea to their first Premier League title?

4. Which manager guided Leicester City to their famous Premier League title in 2015-16?

5. Who was the first manager to win the Premier League in their debut season?

6. Which manager holds the record for the longest unbeaten run in Premier League history?

7. Who is the only manager to win three Premier League Manager of the Season awards in consecutive years?

8. Who was the first Italian manager to win the Premier League?

9. Who was the first manager to win back-to-back Premier League titles?

10. Which Premier League manager has the highest win percentage in the league's history?

11. Which manager led Arsenal to the Premier League title in their unbeaten season of 2003-04?

12. Who was the first British manager to win the Premier League?

13. Which manager holds the record for the most Premier League Manager of the Month awards?

14. Who are the only managers to win the Premier League, FA Cup, and Champions League treble?

15. Who was the first manager to win the Premier League after being promoted from the Championship?

16. Which manager won the Premier League with the highest points tally in a single season?

Category 23:

Premier League Club Nicknames

1. What is the nickname of Manchester United?

2. What is the nickname of Arsenal?

3. What is the nickname of Liverpool?

4. What is the nickname of Chelsea?

5. What is the nickname of Tottenham Hotspur?

6. What is the nickname of Manchester City?

7. What is the nickname of Leicester City?

8. What is the nickname of Wolverhampton Wanderers?

9. What is the nickname of West Ham United?

10. What is the nickname of Newcastle United?

11. What is the nickname of Aston Villa?

12. What is the nickname of Everton?

13. What is the nickname of Crystal Palace?

14. What is the nickname of Brighton & Hove Albion?

15. What is the nickname of Burnley?

16. What is the nickname of Leeds United?

17. What is the nickname of Southampton?

18. What is the nickname of Brentford?

19. What is the nickname of Sheffield United?

20. What is the nickname of Fulham?

Category 24:

Premier League Clubs and European Trophies

1. Which Premier League club has won the most UEFA Champions League titles?

2. Which Premier League club was the first to win the UEFA Champions League?

3. Which club became the first London-based Premier League team to win the UEFA Champions League?

4. Which Premier League club has won the most UEFA Europa League titles?

5. Who scored the winning goal for Manchester City in the 2023 UEFA Champions League final?

6. Which Premier League club won the UEFA Cup Winners' Cup in 1998?

7. Who was the first Premier League club to reach the final of the UEFA Europa Conference League?

8. Which Premier League club won the UEFA Super Cup in 2021?

9. Which Premier League team reached the final of the UEFA Champions League three times in a row from 2018 to 2020?

10. Which Premier League club won the UEFA Cup in 2001 as part of a cup treble?

11. Which Premier League team won the 2008 UEFA Champions League?

12. Which Premier League team won the UEFA Europa League in 2017?

13. Which Premier League club won the UEFA Cup Winners' Cup in 1991?

14. Who scored the decisive penalty for Chelsea in the 2012 UEFA Champions League final?

15. Which Premier League club won the
UEFA Europa League in 2013?

16. Which Premier League club won the
UEFA Super Cup in 1998?

17. Who was the first Premier League club to
reach the final of the UEFA Europa League?

Category 25:

Premier League Clubs and Domestic Trophies

1. Which Premier League club has won the most FA Cup titles?

2. Which Premier League club has won the most League Cup titles?

3. Which Premier League club won the domestic treble (Premier League, FA Cup, and League Cup) in 2019?

4. Who was the first Premier League club to win both the FA Cup and the League Cup in the same season?

5. Which Premier League club won the FA Cup in 2022?

6. Which Premier League club won the FA Cup for the first time in 2013?

7. Who was the first manager to win the Premier League, FA Cup, and League Cup in the same season?

8. Which Premier League club has won the most Community Shield titles?

9. Who scored the winning goal for Leicester City in the 2021 FA Cup final?

10. Which Premier League club won the League Cup in 2023?

11. Who was the first Premier League club to win the FA Cup?

12. Which Premier League club won the League Cup in 2018?

13. Which Premier League club won the FA Cup in 2016, a season in which they also won the Premier League title?

14. Who was the first Premier League club to win the FA Cup three times in a row?

15. Which Premier League club won the League Cup in 2020?

16. Who was the first Premier League club to win the League Cup four times in a row?

17. Which Premier League club has won the FA Cup more than 10 times?

18. Who scored the winning goal for Manchester United in the 2016 FA Cup final?

19. Which Premier League club won the League Cup in 2012?

20. Who was the first Premier League club to win the FA Cup in the 21st century?

Category 26:

Premier League Shirt Numbers

1. Which player made the number 7 shirt iconic at Manchester United?

2. Which player wore the number 8 shirt for Chelsea during their Premier League title wins in 2004-05 and 2005-06?

3. Which player famously wore the number 14 shirt for Arsenal?

4. Which player wore the number 11 shirt during Manchester United's treble-winning season in 1998-99?

5. Who wore the number 9 shirt for Liverpool when they won the UEFA Champions League in 2019?

6. Which player wore the number 8 shirt for Manchester City during their Premier League title win in 2011-12?

7. Which player wore the number 25 shirt for Manchester United for more than 10 years?

8. Which player wore the number 23 shirt for Liverpool during their 2005 Champions League triumph?

9. Which player wore the number 26 shirt for Chelsea during their Premier League title wins in the 2000s?

10. Who wore the number 4 shirt for Manchester City when they won their first Premier League title in 2012?

11. Which player wore the number 10 shirt for Arsenal during their Premier League title-winning season in 2003-04?

12. Who wore the number 8 shirt for Manchester United during their Premier League title wins in 2006-07 and 2007-08?

13. Which player wore the number 11 shirt for Chelsea during their Champions League-winning season in 2011-12?

14. Who wore the number 7 shirt for Manchester City during their Premier League title win in 2017-18?

15. Which player wore the number 10 shirt for Manchester United in the 1999-2000 season?

16. Who wore the number 5 shirt for Arsenal during their 'Invincibles' season?

17. Which player wore the number 6 shirt for Liverpool during their Premier League title win in 2019-20?

18. Who wore the number 22 shirt for Manchester United during their Premier League title win in 2012-13?

Answers

The 1990s –
The Early Days of the Premier League

1. Manchester United

2. Teddy Sheringham

3. Newcastle United

4. Kenny Dalglish

5. Blackburn Rovers

6. 1996

7. Sheffield Wednesday

8. Eric Cantona

9. 2004-05 (Note: though Chelsea's first English top-division title was earlier, their first in the Premier League era was under Mourinho.)

10. Alan Shearer

11. Bayern Munich (in the Champions League final)

12. Brian Deane (for Sheffield United against Manchester United)

13. Les Ferdinand

14. Middlesbrough

15. Arsène Wenger

16. Alan Shearer

17. Tony Yeboah

18. Sunderland

19. Alan Shearer

20. Howard Wilkinson

21. Andy Cole

22. Nottingham Forest

23. Jimmy Floyd Hasselbaink

24. Manchester United

25. 1997

26. Leeds United

27. Tim Sherwood

28. Jürgen Klinsmann

29. Bruce Rioch

30. Erik Thorstvedt (for Tottenham Hotspur)

Category 2:

The 2000s – Rise of the Giants

1. Patrick Vieira

2. Paul Robinson

3. Alan Shearer

4. Chelsea

5. Sporting CP

6. Manchester United

7. Thierry Henry

8. Cristiano Ronaldo

9. José Mourinho

10. 2010-11

11. Carlo Cudicini

12. Thierry Henry

13. José Mourinho

14. Chelsea

15. Fernando Torres

16. Dimitar Berbatov

17. Vladimir Smicer (scored the fifth; Jerzy Dudek saved the last penalty)

18. Manchester United and Chelsea

19. Thierry Henry

20. Harry Redknapp

Category 3:

The 2010s – Dominance of the Top Six

1. Sergio Agüero

2. Leicester City

3. Luis Suárez

4. 2013

5. David de Gea

6. Tottenham Hotspur

7. 100 points

8. Son Heung-min

9. José Mourinho (2014-15) and Antonio Conte (2016-17)

10. Mohamed Salah (shared in 2018-19, won outright in 2019-20)

11. Claudio Ranieri

12. Harry Kane

13. Cristiano Ronaldo (before his departure in 2009, won the award in January 2009)

14. Manchester City (106 goals)

15. N'Golo Kanté

16. 2-0 to Liverpool

17. Fernandinho

18. Mohamed Salah

19. Andy Carroll

20. Virgil van Dijk

21. Dele Alli

22. Alexandre Lacazette

23. Wolverhampton Wanderers

24. Robin van Persie

25. Southampton

26. Harry Kane

27. Tottenham Hotspur

28. Kevin De Bruyne

29. Ajax

Category 4:
The 2020s – Modern Era

1. Manchester City

2. Burnley

3. Kevin De Bruyne

4. Mohamed Salah and Son Heung-min (shared)

5. Youri Tielemans (for Leicester City)

6. Dean Smith

7. Wayne Rooney

8. Mikel Arteta

9. Bruno Fernandes

10. West Ham United

11. Kevin De Bruyne

12. Phil Foden

13. Mohamed Salah

14. Tottenham Hotspur

15. Nottingham Forest

16. Ederson

17. Marcelo Bielsa

18. Youri Tielemans

19. Sergi Canós

20. Erling Haaland

21. Newcastle United

22. Erling Haaland

23. Ederson (Manchester City)

24. Frank Lampard (interim)

25. Erling Haaland

26. Brentford (2021-2022 season promotion, top-half finish in 2022-2023)

27. Michael Owen's record still stands, but in the 2020s, Phil Foden has been among the youngest

28. Pep Guardiola (Manchester City)

Category 5:
Iconic Players and Managers

1. Sir Alex Ferguson

2. Andy Cole

3. Sadio Mané

4. Arsène Wenger

5. John Terry

6. Kevin De Bruyne

7. Sergio Agüero

8. Gareth Barry

9. Harry Kane

10. Mohamed Salah

11. Pep Guardiola

12. David James

13. John Terry

14. Nicolas Anelka

15. Pep Guardiola

16. Ryan Giggs (13 titles)

17. David Seaman

18. Pep Guardiola

Category 6:
Records and Statistics

1. Manchester City (18 wins in 2017-18)

2. James Vaughan

3. Duncan Ferguson and Patrick Vieira (shared)

4. Shane Long (after 7.69 seconds)

5. Kevin De Bruyne (20 assists, 2019-20)

6. Arsenal (49 games)

7. John Burridge (43 years old)

8. Peter Crouch

9. Jimmy Floyd Hasselbaink

10. Peter Crouch

11. Matthew Briggs (for Fulham at 18 years and 65 days)

Category 7:
Memorable Matches

1. 3-2 to Manchester City

2. 9-0

3. Newcastle United

4. 6-1 to Manchester City

5. Frank Lampard

6. Norwich City

7. 2012

8. Leicester City (9-0 vs Southampton in 2019)

9. Dwight Gayle (for Crystal Palace)

10. Mohamed Salah

11. Lucas Moura

12. David Silva

Category 8:
Transfers and Signings

1. Manchester City

2. Harry Maguire

3. Paul Pogba

4. Nicolas Pépé

5. Chelsea

6. Raheem Sterling

7. Romelu Lukaku

8. Manchester United

9. Tiemoué Bakayoko

10. Virgil van Dijk

11. Son Heung-min

1. Manchester City

2. Harry Maguire

3. Paul Pogba

4. Nicolas Pépé

5. Chelsea

6. Raheem Sterling

7. Romelu Lukaku

8. Manchester United

9. Tiemoué Bakayoko

10. Virgil van Dijk

11. Son Heung-min

Category 9:
International Influence

1. Didier Drogba

2. Son Heung-min

3. Tony Yeboah

4. Lucas Radebe (for Leeds United)

5. Didier Drogba

6. Robert Pires

7. 2011

8. Sadio Mané

9. Harry Kane

Category 10:
Premier League Goalkeepers

1. Petr Čech

2. Peter Schmeichel

3. Vito Mannone (for Sunderland)

4. Edwin van der Sar

5. Ederson

6. Tim Krul

7. David Seaman

8. Jens Lehmann

9. Kasper Schmeichel

10. Petr Čech

11. Hugo Lloris

12. Petr Čech

13. Neil Sullivan (for Wimbledon)

14. Tim Krul (for Newcastle United against Tottenham Hotspur in 2013)

15. Joe Hart

16. Alisson Becker (for Liverpool in 2021)

17. Edwin van der Sar

18. Petr Čech

19. Alisson Becker

20. David Seaman

Category 11:

Premier League Captains

1. John Terry

2. Vincent Kompany

3. Patrick Vieira

4. Joe Cole

5. Jordan Henderson

6. Wes Morgan

7. Hugo Lloris

8. Eric Cantona

9. Jack Grealish

10. Tim Sherwood

11. John Terry (though he didn't play in the final, he was club captain)

12. Wes Morgan

13. Eric Cantona (for Manchester United in 1997)

14. Jordan Henderson

15. Patrick Vieira

16. Seamus Coleman

17. Roy Keane (though he was suspended for the final)

18. Conor Coady

Category 12:
Premier League Promotions and Relegations

1. West Bromwich Albion

2. Nottingham Forest

3. Nuno Espírito Santo

4. Reading

5. Brentford

6. Norwich City

7. Aston Villa

8. Swindon Town (1993)

9. Nigel Pearson

10. Burnley

11. Norwich City

12. Marcelo Bielsa

13. Sergi Canós

14. Aston Villa

15. Huddersfield Town

16. Sheffield United

17. Norwich City

18. Blackburn Rovers

19. Swansea City

Category 13:

Premier League Stadiums and Crowds

1. Old Trafford (Manchester United)

2. King Power Stadium

3. Brighton & Hove Albion

4. Manchester City

5. Tottenham Hotspur vs. Crystal Palace

6. Villa Park

7. Newcastle United

8. Craven Cottage (Fulham)

9. West Ham United

10. Everton

11. Old Trafford (Manchester United)

12. Highbury

13. Anfield (Liverpool)

14. Southampton

15. Crystal Palace

16. Everton

17. Emirates Stadium

18. Brentford

Category 14:

Premier League Derby Matches

1. The Merseyside Derby

2. Pierre-Emerick Aubameyang

3. 2-2

4. Roy Keane

5. 1-0 to Sunderland

6. Harry Kane

7. Everton

8. 2-1 to Manchester United

9. Marcus Rashford

10. 3-1 to Liverpool

11. Jonny Evans

12. 1-0 to Arsenal

13. 1-0 to Sunderland

14. 1-0 to Liverpool

15. Pierre-Emerick Aubameyang

Category 15:

Premier League Penalties

1.Alan Shearer

2.David James

3.John Aldridge (for Liverpool against Sheffield United in 1992)

4.Andrew Johnson (11 penalties for Crystal Palace in the 2004-05 season)

5.Teddy Sheringham (for Nottingham Forest against Liverpool in 1992)

6.Leicester City (14 penalties in the 2015-16 season)

7.Matt Le Tissier (scored 25 out of 26 penalties)

8.Brad Friedel (for Blackburn Rovers against Arsenal in 2006)

9.Bruno Fernandes (9 penalties for Manchester United in the 2020-21 season)

10.Wayne Rooney

11.Tim Krul (for Norwich City)

12.Tottenham Hotspur (missed 8 penalties in the 1994-95 season)

13.Ederson

14.Youri Tielemans

15.José Mourinho

16.Mohamed Salah

Category 16:

Premier League Penalty Saves

1. David James

2. Hans Segers (for Wimbledon against Coventry City in 1992)

3. Fraser Forster (for Southampton against Leicester City)

4. Joe Hart

5. Hugo Lloris

6. Kasper Schmeichel

7. Simon Mignolet

8. Adrián (for West Ham United)

9. Ederson

10. Illan Meslier

11. José Sá

12. Nick Pope

13. Łukasz Fabiański (for West Ham United)

14\. Edouard Mendy (for Chelsea in 2021

Category 17: Premier League Goal scorers

1. Alan Shearer (260 goals)

2. Erling Haaland (36 goals in 2022-23 season)

3. Andy Cole (for Manchester United against Ipswich Town in 1995)

4. Harry Kane (for Tottenham Hotspur)

5. Michael Owen

6. Eric Cantona (for Leeds United against Tottenham Hotspur in 1992)

7. Shane Long (7.69 seconds for Southampton against Watford in 2019)

8. Sadio Mané (for Southampton against Aston Villa in 2 minutes and 56 seconds in 2015)

9. Ole Gunnar Solskjær (4 goals for Manchester United against Nottingham Forest in 1999)

10. Nicolas Anelka

11. Harry Kane

12. Frank Lampard

13. Mohamed Salah

14. Wayne Rooney

15. Efan Ekoku (for Norwich City against Everton in 1993)

16. Mohamed Salah

17. Thierry Henry

18. Harry Kane

19. Dwight Yorke

20. Frank Lampard

Category 18:

Premier League Appearances

1. Gareth Barry (653 appearances)

2. Petr Čech

3. Harvey Elliott (at 16 years and 30 days for Fulham)

4. Brad Friedel (310 consecutive appearances)

5. Wayne Rooney

6. Teddy Sheringham (at 40 years and 272 days)

7. Peter Crouch

8. Ryan Giggs

9. Gary Neville

10. David Seaman

11. Ryan Giggs

12. Gary Speed

13. John Terry

14. Mark Schwarzer

15. James Milner

16. Jermain Defoe

17. Ryan Giggs (Manchester United)

Category 19:

Premier League Players' Age

1. James Vaughan (at 16 years and 271 days for Everton)

2. Teddy Sheringham (at 40 years and 268 days for West Ham United)

3. Harvey Elliott (at 16 years and 30 days for Fulham)

4. Michael Owen (at 18 years and 62 days for Liverpool)

5. Teddy Sheringham

6. Wayne Rooney

7. Mark Schwarzer (at 42 years with Leicester City in 2015-16)

8. Phil Foden (at 17 years and 350 days for Manchester City in 2018)

9. Harvey Elliott (at 16 years and 140 days for Fulham)

10. Michael Owen

11. Marcus Rashford

12. Steve Ogrizovic (at 42 years for Coventry City)

13. Danny Cadamarteri (for Everton at 17 years and 345 days)

14. Robbie Fowler

15. Angel Gomes

16. Wayne Rooney

17. Scott Carson

18. Edwin van der Sar

Category 20:

Premier League Players' International Caps

1. Kolo Touré (Ivory Coast)

2. Fernandinho (for Manchester City)

3. Tim Cahill (Australia)

4. David Silva (for Manchester City)

5. Wayne Rooney

6. Cristiano Ronaldo

7. Javier Mascherano (Argentina)

8. Petr Čech (Czech Republic)

9. Mesut Özil (while at Arsenal)

10. David Beckham

11. Eden Hazard

12. Robbie Keane

13. Robin van Persie

14. Darren Fletcher

15. Thierry Henry

16. Eric Cantona

17. Pablo Zabaleta

18. Bruce Grobbelaar (Zimbabwe)

19. Gianfranco Zola

Category 21: Premier League Attendances

1. Old Trafford (Manchester United, 74,000+)

2. 83,222 (Tottenham Hotspur vs. Arsenal at Wembley in 2018)

3. Manchester United

4. 3,039 (Wimbledon vs. Everton in 1993 at Selhurst Park)

5. Tottenham Hotspur (Tottenham Hotspur Stadium)

6. Wembley Stadium (Tottenham Hotspur vs. Arsenal, 2018)

7. 60,383 (Arsenal vs. Manchester United, 2007)

8. Manchester United

9. Goodison Park

10. Old Trafford

11. 42,322 (Chelsea vs. Tottenham Hotspur)

12. West Ham United (London Stadium)

13. 54,693 (Manchester City vs. Leicester City, 2022)

14. Tottenham Hotspur Stadium

15. Burnley

16. 42,788 (Aston Villa vs. Liverpool, 2009)

17. Tottenham Hotspur Stadium

18. Newcastle United (52,389 vs. Middlesbrough, 2009)

Category 22:

Most Successful Premier League Managers

1. Sir Alex Ferguson (13 titles with Manchester United)

2. Pep Guardiola (6 titles with Manchester City as of 2024)

3. José Mourinho (in 2004-05)

4. Claudio Ranieri

5. Carlo Ancelotti (with Chelsea in 2009-10)

6. Arsène Wenger (49 games with Arsenal)

7. Sir Alex Ferguson

8. Carlo Ancelotti (with Chelsea in 2009-10)

9. Sir Alex Ferguson (in 1992-93 and 1993-94 with Manchester United)

10. Pep Guardiola (Manchester City)

11. Arsène Wenger

12. Sir Alex Ferguson

13. Sir Alex Ferguson

14. Sir Alex Ferguson and Pep Guardiola

15. Kenny Dalglish (with Blackburn Rovers in 1994-95)

16. Pep Guardiola (100 points with Manchester City in 2017-18)

Category 23: Premier League Club Nicknames

1. The Red Devils

2. The Gunners

3. The Reds

4. The Blues

5. Spurs

6. The Citizens

7. The Foxes

8. Wolves

9. The Hammers

10. The Magpies

11. The Villans

12. The Toffees

13. The Eagles

14. The Seagulls

15. The Clarets

16. The Whites

Category 24:

Premier League Clubs and European Trophies

1. Liverpool (6 titles)

2. Manchester United (in 1968)

3. Chelsea (in 2012)

4. Chelsea (2 titles in 2013 and 2019)

5. Rodri

6. Chelsea

7. West Ham United (in 2023)

8. Chelsea

9. Liverpool

10. Liverpool

11. Manchester United

12. Manchester United

13. Manchester United

14. Didier Drogba

15. Chelsea

16. Chelsea

17. Fulham (in 2010)

Category 25:

Premier League Clubs and Domestic Trophies

1. Arsenal (14 titles)

2. Liverpool (10 titles)

3. Manchester City

4. Liverpool (in 2000-01)

5. Liverpool

6. Wigan Athletic

7. Pep Guardiola (Manchester City, 2018-19)

8. Manchester United

9. Youri Tielemans

10. Manchester United

11. Arsenal (in 1993)

12. Manchester City

13. Manchester United

14. Arsenal (2002-03, 2003-04, 2004-05)

15. Manchester City

16. Manchester City (2018, 2019, 2020, 2021)

17. Arsenal

18. Jesse Lingard

19. Liverpool

20. Arsenal (in 2002)

Category 26: Premier League Shirt Numbers

1. David Beckham

2. Frank Lampard

3. Thierry Henry

4. Ryan Giggs

5. Roberto Firmino

6. Samir Nasri

7. Antonio Valencia

8. Jamie Carragher

9. John Terry

10. Vincent Kompany

11. Dennis Bergkamp

12. Wayne Rooney

13. Didier Drogba

14. Raheem Sterling

15. Teddy Sheringham

16. Kolo Touré

17. Dejan Lovren

18. Paul Scholes